Working Together Against
GANG
VIOLENCE

Co-founder of the famous California gang the Crips, Stanley "Tookie" Williams is currently on death row in San Quentin State Prison for crimes he committed when he was a gang member. He now speaks out against gang violence so others will not follow his footsteps.

❖ THE LIBRARY OF SOCIAL ACTIVISM ❖

Working Together Against

GANG
VIOLENCE

Margi Trapani

THE ROSEN PUBLISHING GROUP, INC.
NEW YORK

The people pictured in this book are only models; they in no way practice or endorse the activities illustrated. Captions serve only to explain the subjects of the photographs and do not imply a connection between the real-life models and the staged situations shown. News agency photographs are exceptions.

Published in 1996 by The Rosen Publishing Group, Inc.
29 East 21st Street, New York, New York 10010

Copyright © 1996 by The Rosen Publishing Group, Inc.

First Edition

Library of Congress Cataloging-in-Publication Data

Trapani, Margi.
    Working together against gang violence / Margi Trapani.
      p. cm. — (The Library of social activism)
    Includes bibliographical references and index.
    Summary: Informs young adults how to be activists in the struggle against gang violence.
    ISBN 0-8239-2260-X
    1. Gangs—United States—Juvenile literature. 2. Juvenile delinquency—United States—Prevention—Juvenile literature.
3. Violent crimes—United States—Prevention—Juvenile literature.
4. Violence—United States—Prevention—Juvenile literature.
[1. Gangs. 2. Juvenile delinquency. 3. Violence. 4. Crime prevention.] I. Title. II. Series.
HV6439.U5T73 1996
364.1'06'60973—dc20   96-3656
                                           CIP
                                           AC

Manufactured in the United States of America

Contents

INTRODUCTION

A GROUP OF KIDS IS ON THE CORNER,
*hanging out. They're all wearing the same colors, the
same kinds of clothes. They look sullen and mean.
You cross the street to avoid them, and their eyes
follow you.*

*You go to the bathroom at school, and a bunch
of kids are there smoking dope. As you walk in,
they watch you. They tell you that if you tell a
teacher or anyone else, you'll get hurt. You believe
them.*

*Your school has just put in metal detectors. Every
time you enter the school you have to be searched. At
first it feels OK, because you've been worried about
the kids who have guns and knives. After a while,
the kids who have weapons find ways of avoiding
the metal detectors, and you don't feel safe
anymore.*

The increasing availability of handguns is one of the main reasons why gang violence has grown over the past few years.

A group of kids in your neighborhood begins to talk about how people who are different are dangerous, inferior. These kids wear the same kinds of clothes and have the same haircuts. They talk about how people need to protect themselves from "the others who are taking all the jobs, ruining the country." At first they seem like a bunch of losers, but there's something scary about them. You begin to avoid places where you know they'll be.

❖ **VIOLENCE AFFECTS ALL OF US** ❖

Wherever you live, you have probably encountered situations like these. You've seen news reports of drive-by shootings, drug dealers outside and inside schools, metal detectors, kids

7

packing guns. You may even have encountered
these situations in your school or neighborhood.
Sometimes it seems as if no place is safe.

A recent news report points to the frightening
random nature of some of the violence. A young
couple, their small children, and a friend return-
ing from a wedding got lost. They turned down
the wrong street in Los Angeles. They found
themselves at a dead-end in gang territory. Teen
members of the gang opened fire on the car,
killing one of the young people and one of the
children. All this because innocent people were
in the wrong place at the wrong time. In addition to this incident are the frequent reports of
young people killed or injured outside their
homes by drive-by shootings. Often these people
have nothing to do with gangs.

There's so much violence, so much anger, so
little hope. It seems that the only people you can
trust are your friends, your "gang." Over and
over your fears are confirmed by experiences
you have in your neighborhood or things you see
on TV or in the movies. Your parents are also
frustrated by the violence. The police and
others in your community don't seem able to do
much.

Some young people have already experienced
more. Members of the California-based program
Teens on Target talk about how their lives were
touched by violence:

Amy (who will spend the rest of her life in a wheelchair): I got shot in a drive-by shooting. I could have prevented it. My mom was telling me to stay home, but I wanted to go out and run around with my friends instead. I ended up stealing and doing stuff just to be part of the crowd.

Lonnie: I'm an ex-gang member. Basically I didn't care about anything but my gang. My gang was my family. There weren't any programs [in my neighborhood] for me to get into, so I got into the gang. The gang was my life; there was nothing I wouldn't have done for it. I did some things that I can't even think about. I got shot, and I knew the people who put me in a wheelchair.

❖ YESTERDAY AND TODAY ❖

There have always been gangs, but gangs today are different from those in the past. People who have studied gangs, violence, and teens point to several differences.

Christopher Baird, a senior vice president of the National Council on Crime and Delinquency (NCCD), says that there was more juvenile crime in the years from 1970 to 1980 than there was from 1980 to 1990. However, the rates of juvenile homicide have gone up. The NCCD did a recent study on violence that shows that, although overall crime went down from 1988 to 1992, juvenile homicides, or murders, went up by 55 percent. According to Baird, the problem is the availability of guns. "That's a very scary trend. There are a lot of guns in the hands of a lot of juveniles, and they are being used."

Jeffrey Fagan, a professor of Criminal Justice at Rutgers University who has studied gangs, agrees. Fagan says that in the past, problems and disputes were settled with fists, chains, and knives, but today they are more often settled with guns. "It's easier to die. It's easier to get a gun today." Fagan and his colleagues have done a survey of kids in gangs and kids who are not in gangs. One of the questions they've continued to ask is, "Can you get a gun?" In 1985 a third of all of the young people surveyed said yes. In 1993 about half of the kids said yes to the same question. Fagan adds that because of the increased use of guns and the worsening outlook for young people without a good education, the future looks bleak indeed. "There's a common [feeling among] poor kids and middle-class kids, which is that the future is scary."

It seems there are only a couple of choices. You can lie low and hope that you're never in the wrong place at the wrong time. Or you can join a gang for protection and hope that you don't get caught in the crossfire. Neither choice seems right, does it?

There *are* other choices. What we don't generally hear about on the news or in classrooms are young people around the country who are working together with adults and community organizations to stop violence and gangs. Some of these people are former gang members who are looking for a new way to live. Some are concerned citizens who are tired of not feeling safe in their own neighborhoods. Some are people like you who want a better and safer place to live and grow.

This book discusses options and choices you might make to help yourself, your friends, and your community to fight gangs and teen violence.

To find solutions, though, it's important to understand something about the problem. The questions are: What are gangs? Why do kids join gangs? Why are there so many gangs today? And finally, what can individuals and communities do to protect themselves against gangs and violence?

❖ QUESTIONS TO ASK YOURSELF ❖

1) Are there gangs in your community? 2) Are you afraid on the street, in school, or at after-school activities? 3) Do you know people who carry guns? 4) Are there people in your community who are working against gangs and violence?

Hollywood legends such as James Cagney glamorized the life
of gangsters for movie audiences in the 1930s and '40s.

chapter

1

GANGS IN HISTORY

THERE HAVE ALWAYS BEEN GANGS. IN THE late 1800s and early 1900s in the United States, gangsters got together to rob banks and people, and sometimes to protect their "turf."

In the 1800s some of these gangs were formed by former soldiers from the Civil War who couldn't find a job or a place for themselves. Others were formed by people who simply didn't respect the laws of society.

You may have heard of the Jesse James gang, the Younger gang, or even Butch Cassidy and the Sundance Kid. There have even been movies based on their lives. You may have seen movies like *Young Guns*, *Butch Cassidy and the Sundance Kid*, and *Tombstone*. They seem to live exciting lives. But most of these people were killed in shoot-outs or were caught and imprisoned. They were responsible for murdering innocent people who were at the wrong place at the wrong time.

On the East Coast, from the 1800s through

the mid-1900s, particularly in big port cities like New York and Boston, immigrant gangs—often of Italian, Asian, or Irish descent—banded together to carve out their "turf" and to make money. These gangs sprang up in poor neighborhoods filled with citizens who were having trouble adjusting to different customs in the U.S.

In the 1920s and '30s, two new kinds of gangs emerged. There were the small gangs that specialized in daring bank robberies like the Dillinger gang and Bonnie and Clyde, and larger and better organized gangs called "crime families." Crime families, also known as the Mafia and the Cosa Nostra, made large amounts of money during Prohibition. During Prohibition, it was illegal to buy or sell alcohol in the United States but these crime families would sell alcohol anyway. They also demanded "protection money" from storekeepers and business people. If a storekeeper refused to pay protection money, his shop would be damaged by the Mafia and possibly he or his customers would be hurt. They also used blackmail, loansharking, gambling, prostitution, and extortion (forcing small businesses and people to pay them money).

Many of the crime families had their origins in other countries. We've heard the most about the Italian crime families, but gangs also came out of poor Irish and Jewish immigrant communities in Chicago, New York, and Los Angeles.

Unlike gangs in the past who fought their battles with knives and fists, the weapons of choice for gangs today are often box cutters and guns.

Some smaller ethnic gangs came out of the African American and Asian communities in places like New York City, Los Angeles, and San Francisco. Movies portrayed these gangs in the *Godfather* series, *Scarface*, *The Untouchables*. Mention of Asian gangs like the Chinese Tongs were frequent in mystery movies of the 1930s, like the *Charlie Chan* series.

❖ THE ADVENT OF GUNS ❖

In the 1950s, street gangs in large cities concerned law enforcement officials. In those days, the turf wars and violence were easy to avoid if you didn't go to those neighborhoods. White

and Puerto Rican gangs operated in "Hell's
Kitchen," on the west side of Manhattan, and
Asian gangs were found in "Chinatown" on the
Lower East Side of New York City. But in fact,
most of the public didn't see or think about
gangs or gang violence because they were not
exposed to it.

Leonard Bernstein's famous musical *West
Side Story* was a romanticized view of street
gangs in New York City. The musical brought
the issue of gangs to the attention of people
across the country. The two gangs portrayed in
West Side Story—the Sharks, a Puerto Rican
gang, and the Jets, a white gang, were strug-
gling over what each considered to be their
"turf." However, these two gangs fought their
battles with knives and fists. Although the death
of one of the Jets involved a gun, it was clear
that the gun was an unusual weapon and hard
to get at that time.

One of the characteristics of each of these
gangs was that they saw themselves as a group
that needed to defend itself against the rest of
the world. They demanded complete loyalty
from their members and were known to kill each
other over "insults," turf wars, women, and
money. People who belonged to gangs partici-
pated in illegal activities like robbery. Even the
1950s turf wars often centered on murdering the
leader of another gang in order to cripple it.

Among the street and ethnic gangs of the 1950s and '60s, members who lived through the experience often "aged-out." This meant that as they grew to adulthood they began to want jobs and families. During that time, even without a high school diploma, a person could get a job in a factory or other industry that paid well enough for him to change his way of life.

❖ QUESTIONS TO ASK YOURSELF ❖

1) What were the characteristics of gangs in the past? 2) Are there things about gangs from the past that are like gangs that you know about today? How are they different? 3) Do you think it is as easy for kids today to "age-out" of gangs and gang behavior as it was in the 1950s?

chapter

2

MODERN GANGS

IN THE 1970S, '80S, AND '90S, GANGS IN
different areas across the country began to grow
larger and to recruit younger and younger kids.
Kids as young as five and six years of age are
now used as lookouts. The Bloods and the Crips
in California, the El Rukns in Chicago, and
the Triads and Tongs in Chinatowns in San
Francisco, Los Angeles, and New York have all
become known as large, well-organized gangs
involved in illegal activities, including drug deal-
ing, extortion, and robbery.

At the same time, segments of new immigrant
populations including the Vietnamese, Laotians,
and Russians have had difficulty making the
transition to their new home. Some of them
have formed gangs or continued gangs that
existed in their homeland. They formed gangs
because they were "outsiders," and they wanted
to carve out and protect their turf. In that way,
they are not so different from the Irish, Italian,

White supremacist gangs, such as the Skinheads, became more prevalent in the Midwest and other areas of the country in the 1980s and the '90s.

and Jewish immigrants who went before them. Like their predecessors, these groups generally organized around neighborhood turf, ethnic or racial lines, and for protection against other groups.

In the 1980s and '90s, gangs have increasingly organized in the Midwest and other areas of the country around the issue of white supremacy, the wrong idea that Caucasians are better than all other races. The Skinheads are one example. Other groups like the Posse seem to center their activities on sexual crimes and on demeaning young women.

There has been a noticeable rise in female gangs over the past decade.

❖ CHANGING WAYS ❖

In the last twenty years, gangs and gang activity have changed. In fact, the word "gang" has come to be used for a variety of groups that come together for all sorts of reasons. Sometimes these gangs are very small—ten or twelve members. They may not have any organized plan for illegal activity and may not have experienced any threats from other groups. They simply come together out of boredom, out of a need to create a family or to leave their mark in the world.

What distinguishes these groups as gangs is their tendency to become involved in destructive activity: vandalism, petty theft, and minor violence. These groups have sprung up all over the country. They are not limited to any particular racial, ethnic, or economic group. Over the past decade, "girl gangs" have started to appear. Like the male gangs, the female gangs are violent and are often involved in illegal activity.

In fact, today, no community or population remains untouched by gangs and violence. People all over the country feel the pressure from groups of young people who are not in traditional gangs but who are involved in increasingly violent activity. Media reports and stories about gangs, guns, and youth violence are everywhere.

❖ THE DRUG TRADE ❖

At the same time, the larger West Coast gangs have begun to send members to other parts of the country to recruit new gang members and begin gangs in new regions. Their activity is often centered around the drug trade. This began in the '80s and has been growing ever since.

Professor Fagan says, "In approximately eighty-five of the one hundred largest cities today, there are gangs. In forty-two of those cities, gangs have emerged since 1980. What was different about 1980? A number of things. In 1980, the price of crack/cocaine dropped dramatically. There were opportunities for young kids on the street to get involved in selling drugs. Today, many people believe that all gangs are a function of drugs. That is not the case. In addition, 1980 was the beginning of the widest gap in income between non-whites and whites in the history of the United States." Furthermore, it was the beginning of an era in which poverty increased.

"The United States lost well over a million manufacturing jobs in the '60s and '70s," Fagan continues, "and those were the jobs that traditionally working-class kids, whether white, black, or Hispanic, used to get to age-out of gangs and into stable lives.

"There are also tons of middle-class kids in

Gangs members come from all socio-economic and ethnic backgrounds.

Chinese gangs, kids from very strong families with very high income. You can also go to San Bernardino, California, and find tons of middle-class kids in gangs. Middle-class kids from Chicago join the El Rukns. One gang we followed in Chicago started out as a music group. One of their members got mugged by a couple of kids from another neighborhood. They decided the only way to defend themselves was to from a gang."

Gangs have existed in the United States for a long time. People who join gangs come from all backgrounds, African American, white, Latino, and Asian, poor and middle class.

❖ QUESTIONS TO ASK YOURSELF ❖

1) Do you think poverty is one of the factors that encourages kids to join gangs? What other factors do you think contribute? 2) Do you agree that more kids than ever have guns? 3) Why do you think young middle-class people are becoming involved in gangs?

chapter

3

WHY KIDS JOIN GANGS TODAY

ALL PEOPLE LOOK FOR GROUPS TO BELONG to. The reasons are perfectly understandable—to have a group that accepts you, to have friends, to learn from people you admire, and to make your mark in the world as you are becoming an adult. We all want those things.

Teen gangs often come together for many of these reasons, but they have other reasons as well. Many teen gangs are formed for protection against other gangs. Many of the young members are looking for a family that they don't have. Some are born into gang areas and have family members who are already in the gang. Some teens join because the older kids in the gang seem cool, or perhaps they have more money, better clothes, and better cars than anyone else.

"My name is Elvira. I had been in this gang for two years. It's a group of girls, dropouts. We used to

Gangs are groups that come together for a variety of reasons, but who almost always engage in violent and illegal activities.

hang out together for protection. We used to sell drugs. We had like a little business. The guy that supplied us gave us a spot, and he gave us money and stuff so we could get ourselves on our feet. We were like a family—we stuck together. We worked on weekdays from two to nine and on weekends from noon to midnight. One of the gang members is dead now, three are in jail, and four are still selling drugs. I had to get myself out. I got caught, and I was in the system [jail] for five days. I was thinking that I had to change because I was in a hole."

❖ A TEENAGER'S JOB ❖
During your teenage years, according to

youth development experts, you have a big job
to do—you have to make the transition from
childhood to adulthood. To do this success-
fully, everyone has certain needs. Let's look at
some of the needs and supports that all young
people should have. Think about how gangs
might meet some of those needs when others do
not.

Michele Cahill, of the Youth Development
Initiative in New York City, says that young
people will meet their needs whether the community helps them or not. Among the needs
Cahill has identified are an environment that
provides safety and structure, belonging and
membership, which help to develop self-worth
and the ability to contribute, and independence
and control over one's life—the ability to make
decisions about who you are going to be.

Barbara Staggers, a physician at Children's
Hospital in Oakland, California, also studies
teens and their development. "The way you look
changes, the way you think changes, and the way
you feel about things changes. If you are going
through a change in your life and live in a society where everything is changing, where do you
get grounded as a youth?

"I have the pleasure of sitting on a panel
every year at a statewide injury prevention
conference, and I have teenagers with me doing
the talking. They say, 'The most important thing

to us is that you don't invest in us. You talk a
good game, but when it comes to putting the
energy and the effort and the money into the
programs, you don't do it. You don't give us
options and opportunities. You say one thing and
do another. You say, "Don't resolve your
conflicts violently," but that's the way this country resolves its conflicts, I see it on CNN. You
don't spend time teaching me how to become an
adult.' That's what some of them say."

Without community programs, schools that
are interesting and exciting, and parents and
other adults who take time with young people, it
is easy to see why a young person might choose
to be in a gang.

❖ WHERE GANGS FILL THE GAP ❖

For many young people today, parents and
schools and communities are not providing the
support to help young people learn values,
become skilled, and grow into successful adulthood. In earlier years, although gangs and violence did exist, even people who lived in poor
neighborhoods had ways to find support and
opportunities to learn. Hubert Jones, a sociolo-
gist who ran a youth program in Boston,
describes the differences between the world he
grew up in and the one teens are growing up in
now.

"I grew up in the South Bronx in a very poor

neighborhood [filled] with gangs and drugs and all manner of evil. But the social institutions worked. I hid from the gangs in the library. It was an oasis in the neighborhood. All my mother had to worry about was whether I could [get around] the mean streets. Once I got inside a social institution, I was protected, nourished. If I got out of line, there were enough adults to slap me back into line—and believe me, I tried all kinds of stuff. The problem today is that even if you get your youngsters into an institution, you're not sure they're safe."

Psychologist Gloria Johnson Powell agrees and adds her own experience. "There is a great deal of difference between being poor in 1960 and being poor in 1995. I come from a very poor family. I was raised on Aid to Families with Dependent Children (AFDC), but I didn't know I was poor. You didn't have a community that was totally poor or totally wealthy. You had families that were together and structured and functional. You find neighborhoods now that are predominantly poor. You don't find public school teachers living side-by-side with their students, nor do you find ministers and doctors [in some of those communities]. You go to these communities now and major social institutions aren't even there."

Making these differences worse are issues such as the increase in single-parent and two-

working-parent homes. This means that many
young people come home after school to an
empty house. At the same time, the increase in
violence in neighborhoods and across the country makes even the walk home from school a
dangerous thing.

Gangs who are moving into new territories
have become very sophisticated about recruiting
new members. In some areas of the South and
Midwest, gangs have been known to sponsor
"recreation centers" when there are none in a
community. But along with the pool tables and
video games come drugs and prostitution and
violence. Young people turn to these gangs
because they are the only people who seem to
provide something for them.

In 1994, the Carnegie Council on Adolescent
Development program, which studies the
influences that encourage healthy development
in young people, carried out a study. They wanted to find out what happens to teens during
their out-of-school hours and to determine what
kinds of organizations can help teens find goals
and a focus for their lives.

Among the findings of the study, the
Carnegie Council said, "For increasing numbers
of young adolescents . . . instead of safety in their
neighborhoods, they face chronic physical danger; instead of economic security, they face
uncertainty; instead of intellectual stimulation,

An increasing number of young people join gangs because
they face physical danger, boredom, or neglect.

they face boredom . . . ; in place of respect, they are neglected; lacking clear and consistent adult expectations for them, many youths feel deeply alienated from . . . American society. . . Each day, America's twenty million [young people] decide how they will spend at least five of their waking hours (40 percent) when not in school."

❖ WHAT'S COOL ❖

Another part of society influences how people view gangs and violence and what is "cool." That influence is the media—television, radio, movies, and the print media. Ronald Slaby, a senior scientist at the Education Development Center in Massachusetts, has studied the effects of the media on children and adults. "Violence is shown as being everywhere, as being justified, as being rewarded, as being socially approved of, as being heroic, or the essence of manhood. Violence is also shown as being 'clean,' with no consequences. Finally, violence is shown as being an effective solution to solving problems. The real question is why all children don't behave violently after watching lessons of violence portrayed like that."

Esther Ranteria of the National Hispanic Media Coalition relates a conversation with her young grandson that may reveal a little more about the media's effect on our thinking. "He came to me about a year ago and said, 'You

Teens' views of violence are often affected by the video games they play, the movies they watch, and the music they listen to.

know, Grandma, when I grow up am I supposed to be a gang banger?' I said, 'I don't think so. Why are you asking me that question?' 'Well, that's what I see on TV. I see a lot of Hispanics who are gang bangers and in gangs. I saw it on the news again tonight.' "

Slaby and other colleagues like Sut Jhally, a professor at Harvard University, say that part of what is needed to change these ideas is a new curriculum in the schools, including courses on media literacy. Teaching media literacy is teaching young people how to analyze what they are seeing on TV and to pay attention to what messages are being sent through the airwaves.

In areas in the Midwest or the South where gang activity is limited, teens are picking up behaviors, language, and styles of clothing from gangs portrayed in movies and rap music videos. They are adopting attitudes that give off a "tough" or "menacing" image. Some people believe rap music glorifies violence, but that is not necessarily true. Some rap music has anti-violence messages. Rap music can express what young people are feeling and thinking in a way that other musical forms do not. Some people consider rap music the best modern poetry around. But increasingly, the video games that young teens play, the movies that they watch, and the music that they listen to make violence and menacing behavior seem effective, cool, and grown-up.

❖ **QUESTIONS TO ASK YOURSELF** ❖

1) What do you think of what Michele Cahill and Barbara Staggers say about youth development? What else would you add? 2) Do you think Hollywood and the music industry glorify violence and gang behavior? 3) Do you think younger kids are influenced by these things?

chapter

4

WHAT OTHERS HAVE DONE TO HELP

ALMOST EVERYONE'S LIFE IS TOUCHED BY gangs and violence today, whether it's in the neighborhood, at school, or through images on the radio, movies, and TV. The availability of guns, the increase in media images of violence and gangs, and the increase in the numbers of gangs mean that everyone feels threatened.

At the same time, the support that traditionally helped young people grow safely and productively into adults has been weakened. After-school programs, clubs, and other activities for teens are often the first programs cut when budgets are tightened. In many communities today, it's rare that a young person comes home from school to find a parent or other responsible adult there.

❖ YOUNG PEOPLE TAKE ACTION ❖
In Boston, an adult crime-prevention organi-

zation began to look to youth in their communities "to get kids involved in crime prevention and to build civic responsibility." According to program director Marissa Jones, "We felt it was important for the powers that be to listen to teenagers who are living in these high-crime urban communities. We started the program 'Youth with a Voice.' The teens have come up with specific reasons why the police do not have positive relationships with teens. We're hoping to build that relationship between teenagers and officials.

"We had two young men in the program who just loved to draw. I'd see little designs on the conference room walls. I said, this graffiti is too much; we need to channel that energy into something positive. That's how we got the teens involved in developing a crime-prevention comic book, 'Willie and His Hip-Hop Friends.' They really got excited about that piece and did an excellent job." Youth with a Voice distributes the comic book to children in elementary school.

Garry Francis, a seventeen-year-old student, talks a little about his experience when he joined the program. "I came to Youth with a Voice through an anti-violence seminar. The program teaches teenagers how to communicate with authority figures and the media. It teaches them how to express their feelings in a more positive way and to get issues out in the open. It pro-

The East Side Wrecking Squad, a rap group, has lyrics with an anti-gang message.

vides them with non-violent alternatives to solve their problems.

"We [asked] 150 kids about solutions to gun violence. Forty-one percent said we should stop selling guns, stop making guns; 35 percent said there was no solution. With teens having no hope for themselves, we're basically lost as a community. Fifteen percent said there should be more police involvement. Twenty-five percent said there should be more programs and jobs. Most teens are outside doing what they're doing because they have no other place to go."

City Kids Foundation of New York City does a number of things to help young people avoid gangs and violence. One of the activities is a performance group, where young members perform improvisations, musical numbers, and little plays for school and community groups. These performances have positive anti-drug, and anti-violence messages for both young people and adults. Carl Gooding, a member of City Kids, says, "We're a multicultural group based on unifying the races. We're also based on 'safe space.' Safe space is respecting ourselves and our peers. A lot of crime happens because kids have nothing to do, so they go out and rob and steal just for excitement."

Citizens for Safety, another community-based anti-violence organization in Boston, started the first teen-run newspaper in the city, *United Youth of Boston*. The paper is distributed at schools throughout the city.

Sean Fontes got involved with Citizens for Safety through the newspaper. He recounts his first experience: "I was flipping through the *Herald* and happened to see an article about another youth [killed] in Boston. I was surprised to see that the kid was one of my best friends. I had feelings of hurt and confusion, but afterward I felt anger, not just at the incident, but how it was portrayed. I decided to write a story about it. My friend was violent, but not always. I

knew he had his bad aspects. But I also knew his good aspects."

Fontes received a lot of response from the article in the newspaper. "One youth was actually enlightened enough to say he felt he was ignorant, being out in the suburbs. The image he had was that the inner city was a bad place and that if he had to go there he was going to die, just like that. He went on to write a poem about how he was educated and enlightened by us. That was something we also published in our paper."

Lonnie, an ex-gang member who was shot and paralyzed, got involved in the Los Angeles program Teens on Target. He says, "The program is my gang. I could still gangbang in this wheelchair, I could still pull a trigger. But what's going on with me right now is trying to have a solution. My neighborhood now is like a ghost town—everybody locks their doors. I want to bring my community back to life where you can leave your doors open."

❖ QUESTIONS TO ASK YOURSELF ❖

1) Are your friends concerned about guns and violence? 2) Have you thought about problems in your neighborhood? 3) Do you know of organizations in your community that might help? Would a mentor system help at your school?

chapter

5

WHAT YOU CAN DO TO GET INVOLVED

THE MOST DIFFICULT WAY TO CHANGE something that frightens you is to try to do it alone. And the hardest way is to try to do it without knowing what others have done. The first step is to find others who share your concerns and your interest in making changes.

You can begin by talking to your friends about starting a group to discuss problems of gangs and violence in your community. Then ask a teacher, guidance counselor, or local minister to provide a place for you to meet and some advisory assistance. Your school may be happy to sponsor a class project or an after-school meeting. If not, your church or a community organization may be interested. If you already belong to a club or a program, ask the adviser if the group can discuss gangs and violence.

Once you've gotten together, the next steps are to identify the specific problem and the

Discussing the problems of gang violence with your friends is the first step to making changes.

things in your community that contribute to the problem.

❖ SO WHAT'S THE PROBLEM? ❖

A good way to start is to make a list of the issues that concern you. If you don't have gangs in your community but are afraid they may form there, you might start with a list of things that you find frightening. This list might include kids in your neighborhood or at school who carry weapons, or drug use on the streets or in school. Then list the things in your community that you think encourage violence and gang activity, like the absence of activities for young people.

❖ WHO CAN HELP? ❖

List the people, agencies, or organizations in
your community that might give you more information or might help you create a program. This
list might include the local police, churches,
recreational centers, community organizations,
and your school. These are all listed in your
local phone book. You might also find individual
adults who might be willing to help.

❖ WHO HAS DONE THIS BEFORE? ❖

Next, do a little research to find out what
other organizations and communities around the
country have done to stop gangs and violence.
The school or public librarian can help you look
up the appropriate organizations.

Among the types of national organizations you
can contact are Boys and Girls Clubs of America,
the YMCA and YWCA, the 4-H Clubs, the Girl
Scouts and the Boy Scouts, and Girls, Inc. You
can also contact the National Crime Prevention
Council. In addition, the Department of
Criminal Justice has listings of crime-prevention
programs all over the country. You can write or
call these organizations and ask them to send
you packets of information. Several such organizations are included in the back of this book.

❖ USE YOUR LOCAL RESOURCES ❖

Another area you can explore is your commu-

nity's local government: board of education members, the mayor, and police officials. Your group or class can invite representatives to come and speak to you about what they do and what you can do to help insure safety in your school and neighborhoods. Many police departments have special representatives who speak to school and neighborhood groups about safety and crime. You may also want to ask representatives from neighborhood watch groups, safety groups, PTAs, and church groups to join in the conversation with you.

Teens on Target in California brings ex-gang members and victims of violence into schools to talk about guns and violence.

In Atlanta, a group of ex-gang members and older teens started an organization in their schools called Black Teens for Advancement. This organization helps young kids avoid gangs and violence. Among other activities, the older teens act as mentors for the younger teens who are at risk of joining gangs or getting into trouble.

It took a while for these young people to get their schools and their community officials to support what they were doing, but they did it. They are now organizing chapters in other schools and speaking nationally and internationally about their activities. Similar programs exist in other parts of the country. With a little

Some anti-violence programs bring ex-gang members to meetings and schools to talk about guns and violence.

research, you can find programs that will interest you.

❖ ARRANGE A COMMUNITY EVENT ❖
FOR SAFETY EDUCATION

Another step you can take is to ask your principal if you can invite some of the local organizations you've identified to speak to your class or at a special anti-gang, anti-violence assembly. Perhaps you have a teacher who would be interested in helping you organize such an event. If your school is not able to help you with this task, you can approach a church or community center and an adult adviser who would help you.

❖ **CAN OTHER SCHOOL GROUPS HELP?** ❖

Reach out to other groups of students who
might join you. If you have an art club in your
school, ask members to help you create
announcements and invitations for the assembly
or the event. Invite someone from the school
newspaper to attend your organizing meetings.
Think of other groups in your school who
would be interested and ask them to help you
organize events and activities. Your school or
community drama or theater club might develop a performance group with an anti-violence
education message like City Kids in New York.

❖ **KEEP TALKING** ❖

When you are doing your research, you will
find a variety of solutions that communities
around the country have discovered to begin to
combat gangs and violence. Some have organized "neighborhood watches," or "take back
our streets" nights.

Talk to the organizations in your community
and share with them your thoughts on the
issues. Ask them to help you develop programs
to meet those needs. You might decide to issue a
student report on violence that includes concerns, needs and possible solutions. Your adviser
can help you with such a report.

As you go through each step in organizing
your activities, people will have lots of ideas.

Discuss them all. Make sure that the ideas you
agree to act on meet your list of needs and concerns. With each idea that is raised ask, "Will
this help us avoid gangs and violence? Can we
do this with the resources we have in our community? If not, what else would we need?"

❖ COMMUNICATION AND YOUR ❖ SCHOOL NEWSPAPER

At the same time, you may want to explore
how your school newspaper covers these concerns. You could ask the adviser to help you put
together a column about gangs, violence, and
student attitudes toward these issues. If your
school doesn't have a newspaper, see if your
English teacher, the principal, or a guidance
counselor would help you start one.

You may want to suggest a schoolwide survey
on gangs and violence like the one done by
Youth with a Voice.

Some of the questions might be: Do you
know kids who are in gangs? Have you seen violence in the school? Have you been a victim of
violence or do you know someone who has?
What do you think teens could do after school
to avoid violence and gangs? What would make
you feel safer? What can teens do about this?
What can the community do about this? Whom
do you go to when you are afraid? Since some
teens may not want to be known for the answers

Newspapers are an effective way to communicate anti-violence messages. You can make your voice heard by participating in or starting a school newspaper.

they give, you can make the survey anonymous.

Responses to a survey can help you refine the list of concerns and needs you've already developed. They can also help you decide what questions you might want to ask when you speak to government representatives, law enforcement, and youth serving programs when you meet with them.

❖ QUESTIONS TO ASK YOURSELF ❖

1) Do you feel supported by your community? 2) Does your school have a newspaper? If not, can you or your friends start one? 3) Does your community support gun control? 4) Is there a youth organization in your community?

chapter

6

GET THE WHOLE COMMUNITY INVOLVED

IF YOUR GROUP IS INTERESTED IN PUTTING on a larger event, you can ask the principal of the school or the leader of a community center or church to help organize an assembly or meeting around the issues of community safety and anti-violence. Invite police safety officials, community programs, representatives of the PTA and other community groups to join you. Your group can present the results of the survey at that event. You can also ask the school newspaper to cover the event and to do a follow-up column on what the students thought about it.

If you feel that your community is not responding to the needs you've identified, you may want to think about other action. You may encourage students to sign petitions to send to local officials asking them to respond to your findings.

Whether or not you want to organize an event like this one, you can use your school newspaper

The loss of family members or loved ones to gang violence has given courage to people to fight back. Many communities are banding together to make their neighborhoods safe again.

as a way to interview people in programs that have created successful anti-violence, anti-gang activities.

Think about articles you would like to see in your school paper. Think about whom you'd like most to hear from. Are they law enforcement representatives? Young people like you who have gotten involved in anti-gang and anti-violence programs? Representatives of youth programs? Students from other schools who are concerned about the same issues? You may also want to interview local officials for the school newspaper to ask them what they are willing to do.

❖ GATHER RESOURCES ❖

Your group may also be interested in learning more about media literacy and conflict resolution. Conflict resolution enables teens and others to find nonviolent solutions to conflict. Several groups around the country have programs for both of these issues. Ask your school or public librarian to help you find these groups. Several books have been written on these subjects. You may want to sponsor an event based on these issues or ask a local community group to sponsor an evening on conflict resolution or media literacy. Once you've done some research, both of these issues would make good articles for your school newspaper.

These are just some of the ideas you can try to get involved in anti-gang and anti-violence activities. You will find that the solutions that work best are geared toward the specific needs of each community. They usually work because more than one group in the community is involved.

Young people have played important parts in making some of the community-based programs work, but the most successful programs are the ones where young people and adults work together. It may take some time to find the adult or group that can help you get organized. Black Teens for Advancement in Georgia had to go beyond the school system to find adults who would act as advisers. But if you and your

friends get together and want to do something, you will find an adult or an organization who will help.

❖ REACHING OUT IS THE KEY ❖

If you are not ready to form a group or organize events, the most important thing to do is to find other people to talk with who share your concerns and fears.

If you feel alone and don't know where to turn, start with a parent, a teacher, a minister, or another adult who is willing to spend some time with you. An older student whom you respect may be willing to help you.

Many communities have mentor programs where adults who are concerned about young people volunteer their time. Contact the Big Brothers and Big Sisters of America at their national headquarters to find out if there is a chapter in your area. Other mentoring programs may be listed with your local town or city government social service agencies in the phone book. They may also be available through community organizations like United Way, Boys and Girls Clubs, and others.

❖ OTHER SMALL STEPS TO TAKE ❖

Ask your parents to talk with you about safety and your concerns. Tell them you are worried and that you would like to discuss ways to feel safer.

The movie *Boyz in the Hood*, featuring gangsta rapper Ice-Cube, showed many people the dangers of gang violence. If you watch a violent movie or hear a violent song, think about how it appeared: did it seem real, how did it affect you?

Ask a teacher in a social studies, history, or English class whether the class could do a project on preventing gangs and violence.

Ask a teacher or the school librarian if he or she can get information for you on media literacy and conflict resolution. Ask whether they would sponsor discussions about this issue in class or after school.

When you see a violent movie or TV program, or listen to music with friends, talk about how the violence appeared to you. Ask whether it seemed real. Was it the right solution? Who got hurt and why? Talk about how often you see violence on TV or in the movies and whether that violence reflects what you see in your community.

Reach out to other kids who seem to be having problems. Ask them if you can do anything to help. Ask them if they'd like you to help them find a program or adult to whom they can talk.

If you spend a great deal of out-of-school hours alone and don't know what you can do, ask a teacher, minister, or local police officer if there are after-school programs in your community.

Get involved in an after-school activity that allows you to make new friends and learn new things.

Make friends who look for positive things to do with their time. Form a positive "group" that doesn't use violence to get what it wants.

If you are worried, depressed, or can't see a way to get out of a situation you don't like, talk to someone you respect who doesn't use violence, drugs, or negative activity to solve their problems.

Reaching out to the positive people around you is the key. In most communities, there are adults who are willing to help you. Sometimes just starting the conversation can lead you to new ideas and options you hadn't thought of before.

Gangs have a hard time organizing and recruiting in communities where young people are optimistic, involved, and organized. People resort to violence far less often when they know of other ways to resolve their differences, and when they understand the differences between them. You'll also find that setting a series of goals for yourselves and accomplishing even some of them will help you feel more in control,

more hopeful about the future, and less as though the world is a dangerous place.

❖ QUESTIONS TO ASK YOURSELF ❖

1) Do you think the violence you see on television or in the movies affects you? 2) Do you know the meaning of media literacy? 3) Does your school have a conflict resolution program?

GLOSSARY

blackmail Forcing someone to pay money or do something against his or her will by threatening to reveal a secret.

chronic Occurring frequently.

extortion Practice of getting money or other goods by force or threat.

improvisation Practice of performing or making without prior preparation.

loansharking Lending money at illegal rates of interest.

menacing Giving an impression of being dangerous or about to do harm.

mentor Someone who shares his or her skills and experiences with others; a role model or guide.

predecessor Person who goes before; former office holder.

proliferate To multiply in number; to grow rapidly.

social scientist Scientist who studies human society and related topics.

thievery, petty Stealing on a small scale.

turf Territory under a gang's control.

vandalism Intentional destruction of private or
public property.

Organizations to Contact

Activism 2000 Project
P.O. Box E
Kensington, MD 20895
(800) KID-POWER
e-mail:ACTIVISM@aol.com

Boys & Girls Clubs of America
1230 West Peachtree Street, NW
Atlanta, GA 30309
(404) 815-5700

Chicago Commons Association
Youth Gang Drug Prevention
915 North Walcott
Chicago, IL 60622
(312) 342-5330

City Kids Foundation Inc.
57 Leonard Street
New York, NY 10013
(212) 925-3320
e-mail:citykids@aol.com

Community Youth Gang Services
144 South Fetterly Avenue
Los Angeles, CA 90022
(213) 266-4264

Resolving Conflict Creatively National Center
163 Third Avenue
New York, NY 10003
(212) 387-0225
e-mail:rccp@igc.apc.org

Teens On Target
Rancho Los Amigos Medical Center
7601 East Imperial Highway
Downey, CA 70242
(310) 401-8166

United Way
99 Park Avenue
New York, NY 10016
(212) 973-3800

Youth As Resources National Program
National Crime Prevention Council
1700 K Street NW, 2nd Floor
Washington, DC 20006
(202) 466-6272

IN CANADA

Crime Responsibility & Youth (CRY)
Suite 223
151-10090 152nd Street
Surrey, BC V3R 8X8
(604) 559-3888

Victims of Violence National Inc.
Unit 2, 220 Mulock Drive
Newmarket, ON L3Y 7V1
(416) 836-1010

FOR FURTHER READING

Bing, Leon. *Do or Die*. New York: HarperCollins, 1991.

Campbell, Anne. *The Girls in the Gang*. Cambridge, MA: B. Blackwell, 1991.

Huff, C. Ronald, ed. *Gangs in America*. Newbury Park, CA: Sage Publications, 1990.

Mathews, Frederick. *Youth Gangs on Youth Gangs*. Ottawa, Canada: Solicitor General Canada, 1993.

Moore, Joan W. *Going Down to the Barrio: Homeboys and Homegirls in Change*. Philadelphia: Temple University Press, 1991.

Rodriguez, Luis. *Always Running: Gang Days in L.A.* Willimantic, CT: Curbstone Press, 1993.

Rosen, Roger, and McSharry, Patra, eds. *Street Gangs: Gaining Turf, Losing Ground*. New York: The Rosen Publishing Group, Icarus World Issues Series, 1991.

Stark, Evan. *Everything You Need to Know About Street Gangs*. Rev. ed. New York: The Rosen Publishing Group, 1995.

INDEX

ABOUT THE AUTHOR

Margi Trapani is a freelance writer from New Jersey. She has worked in communications for seventeen years. She has directed a program that produces background briefing for the media on youth issues for six years. These briefings combined the latest research with the voices and opinions of teenagers on the issues facing America's youth.

PHOTO CREDITS: Cover photo © Impact Visuals/Lisa Terry; p. 2 by J. Patrick Forden; p. 7 © Impact Visuals/Jerome Friar; p. 12 © A/P Wide World; p. 15 Sarah Friedman; p. 19 © Impact Visuals/Loren Santow; pp. 20, 26 by Elizabeth and Pierre Venant; p. 23 © Image Bank/Butch Martin, Inc.; p. 31 by Kathleen McClancy; p. 33 © International Stock/Patrick Ramsey; p. 37 © A/P Wide World; pp. 41, 44 © Impact Visuals/Donna De Cesare p. 47 by Olga M. Palma; p. 50 © A/P Wide World; p. 53 © A/P Wide World.

PHOTO RESEARCH: Vera Amadzadeh

DESIGN: Kim Sonsky